Court Reform

Law, Governance, and Development

Over a short period of time, the strengthening of law and governance has become a major focus for international development organisations, as well as for governments and organisations at the national level. These are now devoting a substantial portion of development funds into reform and capacity building programmes aimed at legal and administrative institutions in transitional and developing countries.

However, the 'building' of legal and governance systems is proving to be a dauntingly difficult and complex task and one in which the methods of approach are highly contested. It has been assumed that law and governance reform is a technical, managerial and financial matter, which allows for the export of laws and the transplantation of legal and administrative structures. The disappointing results of such reforms have illustrated, however, that not enough attention has been given to how laws, policies, institutions and stakeholders operate in reality, in their socio-political contexts. The uniqueness of individual countries, sectors and institutions is often insufficiently understood, and the actual experiences with the myriad of law and governance programmes and projects are not translated into knowledge on how law and governance reform promotes development.

In response, the Leiden University Press series on Law, Governance, and Development brings together an interdisciplinary body of work about the formation and functioning of systems of law and governance in developing countries, and about interventions to strengthen them. The series aims to engage academics, policy makers and practitioners at the national and international level, thus attempting to stimulate legal reform for development.

Court Reform

Adriaan Bedner

LEIDEN UNIVERSITY PRESS

This Research & Policy Note was drafted by the Van Vollenhoven Institute for the Kenniscentrum Rechtsstaat en Ontwikkeling (KREO). This Centre of Expertise on Rule of Law and Development is a project commissioned by the Netherlands Ministry of Foreign Affairs and set up at the Van Vollenhoven Institute for Law, Governance and Development of the Law Faculty at Leiden University. The views expressed here do not necessarily reflect the views of the Netherlands Ministry of Foreign Affairs.

For further information please contact: Van Vollenhoven Institute, Leiden University: vollenhoven@law.leidenuniv.nl.
This Research & Policy Note is also available at www.law.leidenuniv.nl/org/metajuridica/vvi and the BZ-Intranet.

Cover design: Studio Jan de Boer, Amsterdam
Layout: The DocWorkers, Almere

ISBN 978 90 8728 050 5
e-ISBN 978 90 4850 630 9
NUR 759 / 828

Date of publishing: May 2008

> '[Judicial] reform is exceedingly important work in the modern state. It is also exceedingly frustrating, depressing, infuriating work, and it needs to be said bluntly that it requires exceedingly competent, thoughtful, imaginative people to do it'
>
> *Dan Lev*

Introduction

At present, virtually everyone working in the field of development agrees that the reform of mal-functioning court systems is central in promoting good governance and the rule of law. A properly working court system supports the realisation of many development goals – by protecting human rights, resolving social conflict and implementing state policies. In addition, a substantial scholarly literature argues that courts play an important role in promoting economic growth, mainly by protecting property rights. It is therefore unsurprising that international donors have made available substantial funds for judicial reform, even if neither of these two claims is undisputed (e.g. Dam 2006 and Carothers 2005).

Unfortunately, however, the record of court reform efforts has not been very heartening (Hammergren 2007). Courts seem to be even more immune to reform attempts than executive government agencies. The reason may be that they combine the obstacles common to reform of institutions in the field of public administration with requirements for independence and with dependence on the particular legal culture they operate in. Reformers need to take into account a complex set of relations courts have with other state agencies, other dispute resolvers, and other actors within the state legal system (from the police to solicitors) – but they also depend heavily on such issues as the quality of legislation and legal education.

Three types of reactions to this complexity have been common in court reform programmes. The first response has been a plea for a 'holistic' approach, based on the argument that court reform is impossible if not all aspects of the legal system are addressed at once. For practical reasons this is very difficult, even if the first step – an assessment of the entire legal system – has been made in several cases and can be quite helpful.

Most attempts at court reform, however, have not been informed by sufficient knowledge of the system concerned. This is due to the popularity of the second approach, which could be labeled 'tactical reforms':

ad-hoc attempts to repair specific flaws in the judicial system without carefully considering its relation to other issues (Hammergren 2007: 214-217). An example would be a project that involves introducing time limits into a procedural code in order to reduce delays, which in practice creates a situation where already overburdened judges no longer have time to properly consider a complex case. Since 'tactical' reforms have been the most common type of intervention, millions – if not billions – of dollars have been spent without discernible results (Carothers 2005: 4).

The 'third way' is a mixture of these two approaches, and can be labeled 'strategic reform'. It resembles a tactical approach in scope, but departs from a more careful analysis of the problem in its context so as not to miss important issues that need to be addressed in an effort to affect change (Hammergren 2007: 214-217). If well planned and implemented, a proper sequence of strategic reforms may result in an approach that is fairly 'holistic'.

This Research and Policy Note focuses on strategic reform and the ideas underlying some of the most common elements of such reform. It will discuss the objectives chosen and advantages and disadvantages of the strategies employed to achieve them – if obviously only within the limitations imposed by the scope of this note. The reader should bear in mind at all times that these are insights derived from experiences in particular cases and that they can neither be used as generalisations in any straightforward manner, nor as general prescriptions. The main intention of the paper is to alert those involved in judicial reform to some of the pitfalls and choices related to particular types of interventions.[1] Its concluding remarks will moreover offer some observations on the political nature of judicial reform and on a model that has been developed by Hammergren to promote a proper sequence of interventions for judicial reform.

Strategy Number 1: Promoting Alternative Dispute Resolution (ADR) as an Alternative and an Incentive

The most extreme way of reforming courts is to replace them, and a common approach to this end is to develop alternatives. This has led to a variety of dispute-resolving mechanisms – ranging from mediation to arbitration and tribunals administering justice – under the heading of alternative dispute resolution.[2] Although in Western countries the ADR movement seems to be somewhat past its peak, ADR initiatives in judicial reform in developing countries have continued unabatedly. The main ideas driving ADR have been the following:

- it breaks the court monopoly and forces the courts to become more serviceable;
- it leads to more consensual forms of dispute resolution and increases the likelihood of parties accepting the outcome of a dispute;
- ADR is less prone to become thoroughly proceduralised and tends to be cheaper, more flexible, and faster.

Regarding the first point, both the form of ADR, the actors involved and the type of court cases supposed to be substituted should be of concern. One should question whether ADR offers a genuine alternative, or whether the courts are so difficult to access that parties will settle for ADR in the absence of any other forum for dispute resolution. The danger is that this may force them to use a dispute-resolution system that undermines the position of the weaker party.

Box 1: Lok Adalat

A good example are the so-called *Lok Adalat* in India, which provide an alternative for the official court system. The arbitrator in these cases is usually a retired magistrate, who provides some guaranteed level of knowledge of the law and procedural protection. According to Cranston, the *Lok Adalat* have contributed greatly to the effective resolution of smaller cases, in particular motor cycle accidents (Cranston 1996). However, subsequent research by Galanter and Krishnan has

⇨

demonstrated that the position of poor plaintiffs in these cases has consistently been undermined by the *Lok Adalat*, because the latter simply do not provide the amount of compensation the victim of an accident is entitled to under the law (Galanter and Krishnan 2004).

One may argue that in many cases some compensation is better than nothing, but one should be aware that the availability of ADR in situations such as this one has no effect on the courts whatsoever. In fact, the courts are probably happy to get rid of many cases and will certainly not become more serviceable to potential plaintiffs; on the contrary, they may rather refer victims to ADR straightaway – as indeed has happened in the *Lok Adalat* case. This further reduces the position of plaintiffs, for the 'shadow of the law' wanes when cases on a particular subject are heard no more: the judiciary does not produce case law and hence it no longer provides a clear normative point of reference for disputing parties. In the end, this may undermine state law itself, as it remains unimplemented. The conclusion therefore is that one should pay close attention to the question of whether the form of ADR introduced will be an incentive for courts to reform, or whether ADR more or less stands on its own and should be seen as a full-fledged alternative. Furthermore, one should be aware that ADR cannot provide the same level of rule of law protection as courts are supposed to.

"One should question whether ADR offers a genuine alternative, or whether the courts are so difficult to access that parties will settle for ADR in the absence of any other forum for dispute resolution."

A similar *caveat* applies to the thesis that more consensual forms of dispute resolution are preferable. This depends on the question of whether the acceptability of the decision to the parties overrides the objectives of the state, for instance, the protection of women and children against discriminatory social norms. Promoting ADR may moreover lead to a shift of focus away from the public interest and more toward private issues. And finally, because of its consensual nature ADR can be used as a delay tactic.

Box 2: Environmental Mediation

In a study on environmental mediation in Indonesia, Nicholson gives several examples of polluting firms that had decided to engage in ADR as a means of appeasing the local population without a clear commitment to resolving the issues. Chemical plant *PT Palur Raya*, for instance, entered the mediation process in order to prevent its factory from being burned down by angry farmers. This alleviated some of the pressure being applied on the firm, which subsequently tried to decelerate the mediation process by all means available. In the end the government more or less coerced *PT Palur Raya* into an agreement, but the entire process took several years. In other cases agreements have been left unimplemented to this day (Nicholson forthcoming).

The last proposition – that ADR is less prone to become thoroughly proceduralised and tends to be cheaper, more flexible, and faster – is probably the least problematic. However, it depends on the kind of dispute concerned whether this is desirable or not. As soon as we turn to disputes where basic human rights are at issue, one should begin to question whether ADR should be allowed and whether precisely its lack of procedures does not jeopardise the position of one of the parties involved. Flexibility has its dangers. If we consider ADR in the realm of criminal law, for instance when non-state courts apply customary law, it is not difficult to see that this may be highly undesirable. In fact, it may readily lead to 'vigilante' justice.

"While the literature indicates significant potential advantages of introducing ADR, it depends on its form, the field of dispute resolution into which it is introduced, and the condition of the court system whether these will materialise."

Box 3: 'Linchations'

After the signing of the peace treaties in Guatemala in 1996, serious efforts were made to reform the justice system. One of the efforts made was the promotion of ADR – particularly of customary forms of dispute resolution – which led to what may be called a decentralisation of the administration of justice. In practice, it also led to 'mob

⇨

violence' against perceived criminals, with many petty thieves being shot, stoned, or torn to pieces. In one case the victim of such violence was a Japanese tourist, who was suspected of planning to kidnap local children when she took some pictures of them.
According to Handy, the main reason for these *linchations* lies in the absence of the social cohesion and trust within communities required for indigenous forms of justice or ADR to continue to perform effectively. In the end, the promotion of some forms of ADR when combined with the high levels of violence in Guatemala during the war, has actually paved the way for rather brutal forms of popular justice (Handy 2004, Sieder forthcoming).

In summary, while the literature indicates significant potential advantages of introducing ADR, it depends on its form, the field of dispute resolution into which it is introduced, and the condition of the court system whether these will materialise. The advantages of cheap, rapid, flexible and consensual dispute resolution are countered by a potential lack of protection for weaker parties, a tendency to reduce the impact of state policies by shifting cases away from the courts, and sometimes uncontrolled forms of popular justice. Whether it makes sense to promote ADR thus depends on a thorough analysis of the field of disputes and dispute resolution, and careful consideration of the question what form of ADR may be suitable.[3]

Strategy Number 2: Increasing Professionalism

The second court reform strategy – increasing professionalism – is the oldest and politically least controversial one. Its aim is uncontested: officially every state supports timely, fair, and knowledgeable administration of justice. However, professionalism does have its political side, as it tends to promote judicial independence and – to a lesser extent – accountability among peers. On the one hand this offers an advantage for donors, since projects supporting judicial professionalism may contribute to realising goals that would otherwise remain unattainable – for instance better protection of smallholder property rights – because they go against the interests of the elite in the recipient country. On the other hand, not recognising this political side may ultimately endanger projects, because politically adverse effects seldom go unnoticed by those in power.

"Professionalism does have its political side, as it tends to promote judicial independence and – to a lesser extent – accountability among peers."

Another issue which those concerned with stimulating professionalism are not always aware of, is the vested interests in the organisations themselves to obstruct professionalism. An increase in professionalism may reduce the discretionary powers of judges and other court personnel and thus their rent-seeking opportunities. Awareness of this issue may prevent the same mistakes that were made in the past by donors who assumed that target groups always want to increase their levels of professionalism.

The following section discusses some of the main sub-strategies under this heading.

Reforming case management

This topic has been a 'reformers' darling', as it is a relatively neutral and technical intervention that promises substantial benefits in the field of transparency and reduction of backlogs. Given the proclivity of legal files to get lost, become incomplete, or remain shelved in backrooms, it seems logical to introduce changes to prevent this from happening, which will consequently result in more efficient court procedures.

However, in practice interventions addressing this issue have more often than not failed to deliver on their promises.

Box 4: Computers

This is particularly true regarding the introduction of technology intended to speed up case management. As is now commonly accepted among most donors, introducing computers should be the very last step in a process of reform and not the first. This was not the common sequence in the early 1990s, when, for instance, in Mexico and Costa Rica processes of case management were computerised straightaway. Qualms of excessive bureaucratisation and the same number of staff employed as before have created the impression that these attempts were not very successful (Hammergren 2007: 64).
The experience in the 1990s with computerisation in the Indonesian Supreme Court was far worse, however. Opposition among judges against any increase in transparency ultimately led to a situation where the computers stood idle, with their cables being gnawed away by rats.

The main cause of problems with case management reforms is that they contradict the personal interests of court personnel (e.g. Messick 1999).[4] Accepting bribes to speed up the processing of a case is often a major source of income for court personnel, and thus they remain very reluctant to use technologies and procedures that reduce their ability to manipulate the system. As a result, such changes can only be effective if they are accompanied by genuine incentives for court staff to co-operate – beyond the sheer pleasure of using computers.

"The main cause of problems with case management reforms is that they contradict the personal interests of court personnel."

The key to success in introducing such reforms is in the first place genuine support from the judges, or at least from the leadership of the court. These have the actual means to enforce procedures and if they are not willing to do so, for instance because they are involved in the 'file managing business' themselves, a project of this kind makes little sense. One should also be aware that judges may be reluctant to take action against their staff, in which case not much is to be expected of such reform either (Hammergren 2007: 63).

Another crucial issue is that the technologies and procedures introduced must be properly adjusted to their environment. This seems obvious, but often reformers have been keen on introducing the most novel, accomplished technology instead of more simple, less fashionable ones, that are often better tested and easier to modify. One problem here is that those at the receiving end usually also prefer the latest state-of-the-art tools, which may make it difficult to promote a more pragmatic solution. However, the most sophisticated technologies or management procedures are not going to work in unruly surroundings, where even typewriters are not commonly used yet.

Finally, external pressure in these cases may be helpful to overcome resistance. In particular if courts are large, the court leadership needs to promote an effective system for reporting case management irregularities to ensure that they get proper information on what is happening in their own organisation. This also applies to the judiciary as a whole: if the Supreme Court or a judicial council is willing and trying to improve case management they need accurate data on the dealings of the lower courts. Opportunities for complaints may moreover become focal points for the press to acquire information and thus promote pressure from the media.

Training

Another 'apolitical' issue is judicial training, which probably accounts for its popularity – at least in part. This does not mean that judicial training is unproblematic. The main issue is that donor-funded programmes can seldom, if ever, provide training activities of a structural nature. The result has been that such training is mostly of an incidental nature and will thus have little effect if it concerns general legal training. Moreover, unless changes are made to the institution where the trainees are employed, they will usually not have much opportunity to apply their knowledge in practice.

"Training should fulfil a need; it should not be a reward."

This effect may be exacerbated by transfer policies. Some reports reveal that judges trained in a particular field – i.e. bankruptcy law – may later end up being transferred to positions where their newly acquired expertise is no longer of any use to them. This issue should be taken into account when designing a training programme. The selection procedure for the training is also important, especially if the training takes place abroad. If this matter is left to the receiving party, the programme runs the risk of turning into a travel scheme facilitating short holidays for judges on the verge of retirement. Training should fulfil a need; it should not be a reward.

This is not to say, of course, that judicial training programmes are totally worthless. In particular if new courts or new laws have been introduced, training programmes can be vital for the development of the legal field involved.

Box 5: Commercial Courts

A good illustration of this involves the training of judges for the commercial courts established in Indonesia in the aftermath of the 1998 economic crisis. Sponsored by the IMF, but designed by experts with in-depth knowledge of the Indonesian judicial system, the commercial courts were established to implement the new Bankruptcy Act which was to aid in the restructuring of the massive debts incurred during the crisis. While the courts have ultimately not brought the benefits intended, a thorough evaluation of their judgments has demonstrated that the training they had received in the administering of the Bankruptcy Act had been effective, in the sense that the large majority of cases were decided in conformity with the relevant legal provisions (Bedner 2008: 160-161).

An additional advantage of such training programmes is that the prospect of the training itself, combined with the perspective of broadening one's judicial horizons can become a major incentive to apply for a position on a new court or in a new field of jurisdiction. This, in turn, provides an opportunity to apply stricter selection criteria (Bedner 2001: 203-204).

Furthermore, the scale of training activities is important. Sometimes massive programmes are implemented, but most programmes tend to have a hit-and-run character. Pervasive effects obviously require a much more serious commitment from donor agencies than they are often able to provide.

Box 6: Judicial training centres

An interesting attempt to overcome this problem of scale of training activities has been donor initiatives to establish judicial training centres. In Honduras (USAID) and Sri Lanka (The Asia Foundation) political support for these centres has been less than overwhelming and as a result they have not brought the expected benefits. By contrast, the judicial training institute in Uruguay seems to have fared better. The key here has been structural political support for the entire reform programme, making judicial training a requirement for new judges (Blair and Hansen 1994). The experience in El Salvador has also been rather favourable. An important reason seems to be that in this case USAID had made a thorough assessment of problems in the legal system beforehand. Another helpful detail has been the availability of 'trainers' from the well-institutionalised judicial school in Costa Rica, which reduced linguistic and institutional barriers (Hammergren 1998: 35-42).

A final advantage offered by a training programme is that it can be carried out even in situations where the judicial institution itself is weak, and incapable of sustaining reform. This applies in particular to weak states and post-conflict situations.[5]

Strategy Number 3: Increasing Court Accountability

Making courts and judges more accountable is a major objective of various strategies in judicial reform. While virtually every judicial reform programme aims to increase the level of professionalism, accountability is not often referred to – even if usually the two are closely connected. The main reason is probably that courts are generally averse to accountability mechanisms, which they consider an attack on their independence. This is not only the case in developing countries, for the issue has been hotly debated in many Western countries as well (Contini and Mohr 2008).

There are two reasons why accountability is a particularly salient issue in developing countries. The first is that – unlike in most Western countries – judicial independence in developing countries is often in actual danger. In spite of the third wave of democratisation, developing states are usually still executive-heavy and thus an increase in judicial accountability may provide governments with the tools to twist judicial arms. For instance, performance indicators may be used to remove judges considered politically hostile to the government (e.g. Bedner 2001: 209-210).

"Courts are generally averse to accountability mechanisms, which they consider an attack on their independence."

The other issue is that in many developing countries judicial corruption is a serious problem. Judges here maintain a personal or an institutional interest in subverting attempts to increase their accountability, which they often do by invoking their independence. In this manner 'political' independence is used to foster 'social' dependence, which allows judges to proceed with their corrupt practices.

To summarise, on the one hand accountability mechanisms are important to counter judicial corruption and to increase court efficiency in view of the generally limited resources available to the judiciary. On the other hand, however, they may readily endanger judicial political independence, which must be avoided. Therefore, the question of what forms of accountability mechanisms are suitable needs careful consideration. I will now briefly address the main 'direct' forms of interventions in judicial development programmes to increase judicial independence, and discuss to what extent they can be effective and where the possible dangers lie.

Reform of Procedural Law

The reform of procedural law is a good example of a relatively 'safe' approach to court reform, with the intention of increasing the accountability of the judiciary, making the courts easier to access, and bolstering efficiency. Because red tape in the court systems of most developing countries remains as serious a problem as it is in executive government agencies, simplifying or streamlining procedural laws seems to be an attractive option. Accountability is served mainly through attempts made to increase the transparency of procedures.

The literature reveals two *caveats*, however. The first is that many aspects of procedural law serve to protect the needs and interests of the disputing parties. One should therefore not immediately perceive every apparently formalistic rule as cumbersome only, and before suggesting changes one ought to first explore these needs and interests. This is usually more obvious in the case of criminal law than in civil law, but it is an issue in civil law as well, particularly if power disparities between the disputing parties are wide – not unlike the situation we found with regard to ADR.

"Many aspects of procedural law serve to protect the needs and interests of the disputing parties. One should therefore not immediately perceive every apparently formalistic rule as cumbersome only, and before suggesting changes one ought to first explore these needs and interests."

Box 7: The value of formalism

The first projects implemented under the aegis of law and development in Latin America in the late 1960s and early 1970s, tended to undermine the constitutional protection of citizens which was inherent in the formalistic attitude of judges – in criminal law and in cases against the government. The US lawyers involved in these

⇨

programmes proposed a far more instrumental and pragmatic approach to court procedural law, which may be beneficial when judges tend to take a critical view of the government. However, these judges failed to do so and thus the effect was the erosion of attitudes supporting judicial independence and the protection of weaker parties – in short the opposite effect of what the reformers had intended (Gardner 1980).

The second *caveat* involves the fact that procedural reformers tend to underestimate the personal interest of judges and other court personnel in maintaining intricate procedural rules. Simply put, these rules and regulations enable them to benefit financially. Although perhaps morally reprehensible, this tends to be a relatively benign form of corruption. Given the generally under-funded state of courts in developing countries, their employment of the opportunities offered by strict procedures to help expedite the passage of a case is not nearly as problematic as the actual acceptance of bribes to produce a favourable judgment.[6] It shows once again that one must be careful not to approach typically legal reforms as isolated cases. Instead one should evaluate their role and function in the organisation and informal workings of the court. Procedural change may very well lead to more serious and uncontrollable forms of corruption.

Nonetheless, reforms in procedural law may be highly beneficial to the weaker parties in disputes without endangering legal certainty. This applies in particular to laws governing the admission of evidence in civil and administrative courts. Good examples include the fields of consumer and environmental law, where evidentiary rules very often restrict those seeking redress of injustices.

Box 8: Evidential formalism

Often accused of being excessively formal, Indonesian judges indeed sometimes demonstrate an extreme preference for documentary evidence. A good example are pollution cases, where the victims are generally urban poor or small peasants. Judges usually dismiss their testimony concerning foul-smelling, strangely coloured water, illnesses contracted after bathing in a river, and rice fields that no longer yield a harvest – instead they will demand as evidence administrative warnings issued by the executive and sampling outcomes based on strict procedures. In many other countries the burden of proof in such cases is shifted to the supposed polluter, who is required to record

⇨

the amount of sludge produced and demonstrate how he has disposed of it. The introduction of this regulation in Indonesia would greatly benefit the position of plaintiffs in such cases, but also positively effect environmental law enforcement more generally (Bedner 2007).

Such changes do require sound knowledge of the situation at hand, but the danger that their implementation will backfire is considerably smaller than in cases involving sweeping reforms of procedural law. Once again, the key to success and the reduction of risks involves a thorough knowledge of both the law and the practice it sustains.

Publication of judgments

The two most traditional forms of promoting judicial accountability are the openness of the court and the publication of judgments. Openness of the court is seldom mentioned in the literature as a serious problem, with the exception of cases allegedly involving state security. However, publication of judgments is a problem in many countries.

Sometimes the situation has deteriorated to the extent that court judgments are no longer even considered as something that should be available to the general public, but instead are perceived as private documents belonging to the disputing parties – who in the worst of cases do not even get the judgment themselves (Pompe 2005: 435-441).[7]

The situation is clearly most problematic when it concerns judgments made by the highest judges. This has consequences that reach far beyond the mere interest of the parties involved in the case, as it disempowers the 'forum of jurists' to supervise and criticise legal developments and affects the very nature of legal education.

Box 9: The role of case law

While differences between common and civil law jurisdiction tend to be exaggerated, this problem seems indeed more widespread in countries with a civil law heritage. The common law legal education instils judge with such an aversion for statutes while exalting their own, judge-made law, that eliminating case law really flies in the face of everything they stand for. By contrast, civil law jurisprudence, with its emphasis on statutory law, tends to make judges less concerned about the general availability of case law. Moreover, the common law

⇨

heritage has created an international forum, where judges and other lawyers critically follow the development of jurisprudence in other common law jurisdictions. This is most evident in cases where the judiciary is pressured by the executive. For example, when Pakistan's Chief Justice Chaudry was dismissed it not only led to an outcry from fellow judges, but from the entire legal profession as well. This may seem somewhat unrelated to the issue of the publication of judgments, but case law is one of the main focal points of the legal professions and legal education. The absence of case law leads to the severing of the oversight function of jurists and the 'common bond' between lawyers in general that is inherent in shared understandings of the law.

Moreover, a situation where case law is not generally available is detrimental to legal certainty and consequently increases the discretionary powers of judges. In short, this particular issue should be a major concern of judicial reform.

Within the judiciary, oversight that involves the evaluation of judgments is obviously another matter. Appellate courts do get to evaluate judgments and may therefore promote unification. However, the greater the number of courts within one system, the more judges sitting in the highest court and the greater the backlog of cases, the more difficult it becomes to maintain some form of unity.

"a situation where case law is not generally available is detrimental to legal certainty and consequently increases the discretionary powers of judges."

Box 10: Indian backlogs

In 2003 the widely respected Supreme Court of India, composed of 26 judges, was struggling with a backlog of 20,000 cases, one Indian Supreme Court judge disposing of more than 2000 cases annually. When in 2007 the backlog had increased to more than 40,000 cases, the government proposed to raise the number of judges from 26 to 30 (Bill no. 41 of 2008).
However, the seriousness of this situation is small compared to India's 18 High Courts which in 2003 were faced with a backlog of more than three million cases (Krishnan 2003).
It will be clear that under such conditions higher courts can hardly offer any clear guidance to lower courts by means of case law.

One should be aware that data concerning the uniformity in judging are scant almost everywhere. Cases are often randomly selected for publication on the basis of unclear criteria and generally speaking one may safely conclude that there is a serious knowledge gap regarding actual court performance from a legal point of view.[8] The availability of computers means a potential revolution in this situation, and may very well lead to a major impetus for reform – if indeed such a system can be instituted.

Box 11: Uploading Supreme Court decisions

With support of several donors, including AusAID and the EU, Indonesia's Supreme Court has now adopted a system where every judgment passed will be automatically uploaded onto the Supreme Court website. As a result anyone who is interested can access them and thus an enormous amount of information on the state of Indonesian legal reasoning has become available. The main reason this effort has not ended up like the situation that occurred in the 1990s (see box 4) is that the Supreme Court leadership has supported this move. The challenge now is to make selections from this massive amount of data so that it can be used for the discussion of legal developments in the literature and for teaching purposes. This should eventually revolutionise Indonesian legal education, which currently focuses mainly on statutory law and cases from prior to 1975.

Of course one should in this case as with procedural changes, never underestimate how vested interests may ultimately block attempted reform. Not only are judges often unwilling to submit themselves to external scrutiny, many academics may be averse to writing articles and adjusting their teaching methods because this will divert their energies from side jobs which allow them to earn often badly needed extra income. In short, related fields, such as education, need to be reformed as well in order to acquire the benefits of publication of judgments.

"Never underestimate how vested interests may ultimately block attempted reform."

Recruitment

The recruiting of new judges is an issue that donors involved in reform programmes can usually only address peripherally, but sometimes their programmes provide them with the leverage needed to influence recruitment practices. One of the most promising ways to use this opportunity has been to open up the judiciary to non-career judges.

This matter is of vital interest in the context of judicial accountability, as it introduces candidates from outside the judiciary to positions within, which may lead to new forms of professional accountability. In particular in countries from the civil law tradition judiciaries have traditionally been closed shops, composed of career judges who have been drawn directly from graduates of the universities. In this regard, the generally stronger professional bonds between the public and private legal professions in countries with a common law background often provide a more favourable point of departure.

"It introduces candidates from outside the judiciary to positions within, which may lead to new forms of professional accountability."

One should be aware of the general aversion that career judges have to allowing outsiders into their ranks. This may even lead to judges employing cunning legislative tactics to prevent such access.

Box 12: Resistance against outsiders

The first case involving the Indonesian judiciary being exposed to a regime that allowed the recruitment of non-career graduates were the Indonesian administrative courts, established in 1991. For the first time non-career judges could be appointed, despite protests from the judges' trade union during hearings in Parliament. In practice, however, this provision has remained a dead letter, because the main drafter of the law – a judge himself – made sure that regardless of the professional experience of the outsider the latter would have to start his judicial career at the bottom in the lowest court. (Bedner 2001: 199 n. 39)

A more common problem is that judicial salaries are usually so unattractive when compared to those in the higher echelons of the private legal profession that it becomes difficult to attract candidates from this pool. A potential solution is to allow outsiders to serve as judges-in-ad-hoc. There have been positive experiences with this option, for instance in the case of the human rights court and the corruption court in Indonesia (Cammack forthcoming, Tahyar forthcoming).

Generally speaking, the possibilities to open up courts to outsiders are better in cases involving newly established courts than in more traditional or settled ones. The best example is probably the constitutional courts which have spread rapidly across the globe in recent years and which usually include judges from a variety of backgrounds (e.g. Ginsburg 2003).

The other side of this coin is that if it is not handled with some circumspection, allowing outsiders to be appointed to higher positions in the court system creates a situation where the judiciary is easily manipulated and corrupted. In particular the appointment of chief justices by the executive may be used as a shortcut to gaining control of the judiciary. It is no coincidence that the procedure regarding the appointment of Justices at the US Supreme Court is heavily politicised and includes numerous checks and balances. Unfortunately, the list of examples of the manipulation of nomination procedures for supreme court appointments around the world is long and dismal.

Career Management

In the previous section we have already touched on some of the issues concerning judicial careers. Career management in the judiciary is particularly sensitive because of its relation with judicial independence and judges' aversion to being held accountable other than via official forms of appeal. The question is whether appeals yield sufficient insight into the competence of individual judges as a basis for career management. Especially if justice is administered by councils of judges, it becomes quite difficult to assess the individual capacities of the judge.

The consequence of not having the proper means of evaluating an individual judge's performance, is that the only people aware of an individual judge's abilities are his fellow colleagues. The chairman of the court in particular assumes a central position in career management, as he is usually the one on whose information those in charge of judicial career management rely. In order to prevent this classic principal-agent situation from developing, alternatives are necessary to avoid this type of a monopoly of information.[9]

One of the most remarkable developments in this field is the rapid proliferation of judicial councils. The main reason for their popularity is that they are supposed to be more suitable for managing judicial careers than ministries of justice, because, as separate institutions, they are more independent of government influence. At the same time, they may prevent supreme courts from having to fulfil various management tasks for which the latter are not fully equipped. However, in some cases an important reason for their establishment has been that the supreme courts themselves are deemed so corrupt that they cannot be entrusted this task.

The difficulty with evaluating the performance of judicial councils is that they differ so much in composition and function. While some are solely concerned with the selection of supreme court candidates or investigating corruption charges, others control the entire judicial transfer system. Again, which tasks can better be performed by a special body other than the supreme court or the ministry of justice greatly depends on the situation in the country concerned.

"Understanding career systems is not only important when deciding on the kinds of interventions that may actually lead to improvements, but also for understanding how judicial corruption works."

A particular problem for judicial councils in managing judicial careers is that they have even greater difficulties in gaining insight into the capacities of judges than supreme courts. An obvious first step would be to evaluate judgments, but as we have seen in many systems it is difficult to link judgments to individual judges. This means that in order to function effectively judicial councils need an entire set of criteria and tools to assess judicial performance. Moreover, the leading systems of judiciary quality management – those developed in the US and the Netherlands – evaluate courts, not judges. The external evaluation of individual judges is highly controversial and risky.

Understanding career systems is not only important when deciding on the kinds of interventions that may actually lead to improvements, but also for understanding how judicial corruption works. While there seems to be a basic recognition that low salaries among the judiciary leads to susceptibility of illicit payments, the link to career management is not always made. If judges are transferred from one court to another or from one part of the country to another, there is a serious probability that corruption schemes have come into existence which enable judges to influence this process. In other words, judges pay for a transfer to an 'attractive' court. A clear system of rules and requirements may hinder this process, but is unlikely to fully curb it.

The main consequence of such an illicit transfer system is not only that it diverts attention from merit-based criteria, but also that it reinforces 'ordinary' corruption. In order to raise the amounts of money needed for a favourable transfer, judges inevitably seek extra money from litigants. The system is not unlike tax farming, but then in a more illicit form. In order to reform this realm, one needs to be aware of the informal ranking of courts before effective measures can even be considered.

Court monitoring

A useful development for aiding in the resolution of problems concerning the accountability of courts has been the establishment of special 'court watch' institutions. Their activities consist of monitoring proceedings in selected cases in selected courts, and their mere presence may influence the approach taken by judges.

While helpful in principle, budget limitations constitute a significant barrier to the effectiveness of court watch institutions. A careful selection of cases is essential, as otherwise their influence will be negligible. Their potential effectiveness further depends on the accessibility of court decisions. If these are available, the ambit of their activities may become much wider.

Another important factor is the possibility for such organisations to co-operate with other NGOs, which may provide them with important data on the cases concerned. Operating on their own, they run a serious risk of having to reinvent the wheel and spend large amounts of time and effort on gaining knowledge of basic legal issues underlying the cases they look at. A reportedly helpful alternative is the involvement of retired judges, prosecutors or solicitors in their activities.[10]

Concluding remarks

This Research & Policy Note has attempted to point out some of the pitfalls connected to interventions aimed at improving judicial performance, or promoting ADR. As stated at the outset, its intention has not been to provide a concise guide to judicial reform, but to alert those involved in reform efforts to certain linkages between topics not always considered as interconnected.

Rather than rehashing all of these suggestions once again, this final section lists a few general points concerning the decision-making process of whether to start a judicial reform programme or not, and the 'sequence' that should be followed by those involved in such projects in order to maximise their effectiveness.

The first point is that to a large extent the political situation determines the kinds of interventions that may be successful. Recent studies on new constitutional courts have indicated that these courts can only be established in democracies with some likelihood of the government being replaced by its political opponents after the next elections (Ginsberg 2003). Similar arguments may apply to courts on a broader level. If a government is unsympathetic to judicial reform, there is no chance of introducing sweeping changes, unless significant political opposition can be mounted against such a government. Of course, donor interventions themselves can be part of that clout, but for a donor to make such a decision requires a considerable amount of knowledge of the political situation beforehand.

The second point is that as any other organisation judiciaries, like fish, 'rot from the head', and their renewal should begin from the top down as well. Irrespective of the political situation, if the leadership of the judiciary blocks reform little is likely to happen and the replacement of the resistant leadership in that case should override all other concerns. On the other hand, it may be wise in such situations to invest in judges on the lower parts of the courts' hierarchy while waiting for higher level changes to occur, as otherwise no alternative infrastructure will be available for court reform when the windows of opportunity start to open.

The third and final point is the matter of sequencing. We have already paid some attention to this, but its importance cannot be overestimated. The following list developed by Linn Hammergren after a long career in judicial reform provides an excellent device for this purpose:

Box 13: Sequencing

Step 1 – Knowledge Building and Application as an Input to Goal Definition
Step 2 – Constructing Demand and Designing Interventions and Objectives around an Adequate Knowledge Base
Step 3 – Strengthening Organizational Capacity for Self-Regulation
Step 4 – Increasing Internal Efficiency and Attacking Traditional Vices
Step 5 – Increasing Efficacy by Differentiating Tasks
Step 6 – Reconsidering the Organizational Mandate and Alternatives for Handling It
Step 7 – Taking on New Tasks and Redefining the Organizational Clientele
Source: Hammergren 2007

According to its author, the above scheme does not claim that every step has to be completed before the next one can be started. Depending on the goals of the reform, steps may be taken simultaneously or be skipped altogether. Nonetheless, the order is logical and should be consulted when considering any reform. And finally, the first step is indispensable in any attempt at judicial reform. Too often has it been forgotten, and too often has this led to the failure of entire programmes. Not taking this lesson to heart may endanger the entire endeavour of donor-supported judicial reform.

"If it is based on sound knowledge and carried out by capable people, under relatively favourable conditions, a strategic, small-step and long-term approach will ultimately make a difference."

And this point brings us full circle. As the opening quote by Dan Lev stated, judicial reform is both exceedingly important and exceedingly difficult. This Note has outlined a number of reasons for such difficulties and has further demonstrated that there is no shortcut one-model-fits-all solution when it comes to judicial reform. However, if it is based on sound knowledge and carried out by capable people, under relatively favourable conditions, a strategic, small-step and long-term approach will ultimately make a difference.

Notes

1 The reader will also find that most of the examples are drawn from Indonesia, as the author of this note has worked on issues concerning the Indonesian judiciary extensively, and is best acquainted with the cases in this country. Nonetheless, the issues discussed are not specific to Indonesia.

2 For an overview of various forms of dispute resolution and the place of courts in this spectrum, see Shapiro 1986, in particular pp. 1–8.

3 Recently the notion of 'Access to Justice' has replaced ADR as a more popular approach in judicial reform. Unlike ADR, Access to Justice does include common forms of court procedure, but more broadly conceived it covers many of the ADR mechanisms. There is a danger here that this will go unnoticed, and that that some of the lessons to be learned from ADR will not be taken into account in Access to Justice. Looking beyond labels will hopefully prevent this from happening. On Access to Justice, see VVI/KREO Research and Policy Note on "Access to Justice and Legal Empowerment: Making the Poor Central in Legal Development Co-operation", February 2008.

4 This usually includes judges, but it depends on the particular constellation of the court concerned.

5 An example of this is the programme sponsored by UNDP and the World Bank in Sudan.

6 This is of course different in the case of courts performing administrative functions, such as legalising birth certificates or divorce, but it is crucial to the performance of courts as dispute resolvers.

7 There may be conscious court politics to delay the publication of judgments. A good example is the recent judgment of the Indonesian Supreme Court of former President Soeharto v. Time, ordering the latter to pay almost 100 million US dollars for defamation, which was sent to the defendant more than a year after it had been passed.

8 Of course advocates who find that their case has been dealt with differently than expected may address this matter in public.

9 For examples see Contini & Mohr 2008.

10 Personal communication from ms. N. Colbran, official of the Indonesia Programme of the Norwegian Human Rights' Institution (10-4-2008).

References and Suggestions for Further Reading

Bedner, A. W. (2001), *Administrative Courts in Indonesia: A Social Legal Study*, The Hague, London, Boston: Kluwer Law International.

Bedner, A.W. (2007) 'Access to Environmental Justice in Indonesia', in: Harding, A. (ed.) *Access to Environmental Justice*, The Hague, London, Boston: Kluwer Law International, pp. 89-123.

Bedner, A.W. (2008) 'Rebuilding the Judiciary in Indonesia: The Special Courts Strategy', in HiiL, 'Further Conceptualization and Practical Progress on Building Coherent and Effective Rule of Law Programmes and Strategies', Papers' Binder, pp. 147-164.

Cammack (forthcoming) 'The Indonesian Human Rights Court', in: Harding, A. and P. Nicholson, *New Courts in Asia*, London, Ashgate.

Carothers, Thomas (2006) 'The Rule of Law Revival', in: Carothers, Thomas (ed.), in: Carothers, Thomas (ed.), *Promoting the Rule of Law Abroad: the Problem of Knowledge*, Rule of Law Series, Vol. 34, Washington: Carnegie Endowment for International Peace, pp. 15-30.

Cranston, R. (1996) 'Access to justice in South and Southeast Asia', in: Faundez, J. (ed.) *Good Government and Law: Legal and Institutional Reform in Developing Countries*. London: St. Martin's, pp. 233-257.

Dam, K.J. (2006) *The Law-Growth Nexus: The Rule of Law and Economic Development*. Washington D.C.: Brookings Institution Press, 2006.

Galanter, M.S. and Krishnan, J.K. (2004) 'Bread for the Poor: Access to Justice and the Rights of the Needy in India', *Hastings Law Journal*, Vol. 55, pp. 789-834.

Gardner, J.A. (1980) *Legal Imperialism: American Lawyers and Foreign Aid in Latin America*, Madison, University of Wisconsin Press.

Ginsburg, Tom (2003) *Judicial Review in New Democracies: Constitutional Courts in Asian Cases*, Cambridge, Cambridge University Press.

Hammergren, L. (2007) *Envisioning Reform: Improving Judicial Performance in Latin America*, Pennsylvania, The Pennsylvania State University Press.

Handy, J. (2004) 'Chicken Thieves, Witches, and Judges: Vigilante Justice and Customary Law in Guatemala', *Journal of Latin American Studies*, Vol. 36, pp. 533-561.

Krishnan (2003) Social Policy Advocacy and the Role of the Courts in India, *American Asian Review,* Vol. 21, no. 91, available at SSRN: http://ssrn.com/abstract=682326.

Messick, R.E. (1999) 'Judicial Reform and Economic Development: A Survey of the Issues', *World Bank Research Observer* 14, pp. 117-136.

Nicholson (forthcoming) *Environmental Dispute Resolution in Indonesia,* Leiden, KITLV Press.

Shapiro, Martin (1986) *Courts: A Comparative and Political Analysis,* Chicago, University of Chicago Press.

Sieder, R. (forthcoming) 'Legal Globalization and Human Rights: Constructing the 'Rule of Law' in Post-Conflict Guatemala', in: Pitarch, P., Speed, S. and X. Leyva (eds.) *Human Rights in the Maya Region: Global Politics, Moral Engagements and Cultural Contentions,* Duke University Press.

Tahyar, B. (forthcoming) 'The Anti-Corruption Court in Indonesia', in: Harding, A. and P. Nicholson, *New Courts in Asia,* London, Ashgate.

About the Author

This Research & Policy Note was written by Adriaan Bedner, senior lecturer at the Van Vollenhoven Institute for Law, Governance and Development at Leiden University.

The author wants to thank Ineke van de Meene, Theo Veenkamp and Dory Reiling for their constructive comments.

Printed in Dunstable, United Kingdom

91228671R00020